Cool Board Sports

Happy House

About Wise & Wide

- A systematic 6-level English reading program based on Lexile® measures
- Diverse and interesting topics chosen from the elementary curriculums of Korea and English speaking western countries
- Well-written books in various forms including fiction stories, descriptive texts, and classics retold
- The informative but original fiction stories grab your interest, leading to the easy and clear understanding of the educational content.
- Improve thinking skills with solid after-reading activities at all levels of the series.

Wise & Wide is a 6-level English reading program that consists of 60 books and each level is systematically divided by Lexile® measures. The Lexile® Framework for Reading is the most popular reading measuring system in American formal education curriculums and many English programs. Over 20 out of 50 states in the U.S. mark Lexile® measures directly on students' final report cards and over 300 well-known publishers adopt and use Lexile® measures.

Experience many kinds of readings written by professional writers from the U.S. and England. They used interesting topics that were carefully chosen after analyzing elementary curriculums from around the world including Korea, the U.S., England, and Australia among many others. Comprehensive after-reading activities including graphic organizers, speaking tasks, and After-reading Tests are ready for you.

Levels in the series and their corresponding Lexile® measures

Level	Lexile® measures	U.S. Grade
Level 1	Below 200L	Pre K - K
Level 2	190L - 400L	Lower Grade 1
Level 3	350L - 530L	Upper Grade 1
Level 4	420L - 650L	Grade 2
Level 5	520L - 940L	Grade 3 - 4
Level 6	830L - 1070L	Grade 5 - 6

* Smart Readers: Wise & Wide level 1 is applicable to the preschool level in the U.S.

* The source of the relationship between Lexile® measures and U.S. school grades: CCSS(Common Core State Standards) FOR ENGLISH LANGUAGE ARTS, APPENDIX A (2012, which is used by 45 states in the U.S.)

Topic List

	Level 1	Level 2	Level 3	Level 4	Level 5	Level 6
Book 1	Science>Biology: The hibernation of animals Story	Science>Biology: Living and nonliving things Story	Science>Biology: Animals & the Environment: Sea otters Story	Environment> Living with nature: The diver & the persimmon tree Story	Science>Biology: Animal: Amazing animals of the Amazon Story	Science>Biology: Germs, transmitted diseases Story
Book 2	Literature> World classics: Aesop's fables Story	Literature> Traditional fairy tale: Old tales about stones Story	Social Studies> Economy: To run a business to make and save money Story	Science>Biology> Plants: Photosynthesis Story	Science>Earth science: Earth's layers earthquakes, volcanoes, and earth's atmosphere Report	Mathematics> Sequence: The golden ratio & the Fibonacci sequence Story
Book 3	Science>Physics: How shadows are formed Story	Literature> World classics: Peter Pan Story	Science>Scientific technology: Nanobots Story	Literature>Myths: World's creation stories Story	Literature> Legend: The story of King Arthur Story	Literature>Myths: Constellation myths Story
Book 4	Literature> Traditional literature: The Talmud Story	Science>Biology> Animal: Polar bears Story	Science>Biology> Animal: Mountain gorillas Story	Social Studies> Cultural anthropology: Amazing ancient cultures of the world Story	Science> Earth science: Clouds and weather Story	Literature> Human & animals: The friendship between a girl and a horse Story
Book 5	Social Studies> Ethics: Rules in daily life Story	Science>Biology> The five senses Report	Social Studies> Cultural anthropology: Astonishing festivals Report	Art>Music: Stories from two operas Story	Social Studies> World culture & history: The Renaissance Story	Sports> Board sports: Surfing & snowboarding Story
Book 6	Social Studies> World geography & travel: Tourist attractions around the world Story	Science>Biology> Animal: Dinosaurs Story	Science> Astronomy: The solar system Story	Social Studies> People: Three great people who overcame hardships Story	Science>Scientific technology: The wonderful world of robots Report	Art>Music: Composers of the Romantic Era Report
Book 7	Science> Space science: The life of astronauts Report	Social Studies> Cultural anthropology: Mythological monsters from around the world Report	Mathematics> Elementary mathematics: Numbers, measurement, shapes and data Report	Science & Social Studies> Technology & culture: Inventions from around the world Report	Art>Works of art: Famous paintings Report	Social Studies> Human & animals: Animals in action for human Report
Book 8	Social Studies> Cultural anthropology: Various living cultures of the world Story	Art>Music: Instruments in the orchestra Story	Social Studies> Life safety: Learning and using outdoor survival skills Story	Social Studies> History: The California Gold Rush Report	Social Studies & Science> Psychology: Psychology in everyday life Story	Literature> World classics: The Merchant of Venice Story
Book 9	Social Studies> Jobs: Interviews about jobs Report	Science>Scientific technology: Developments in technology in different times Story	Social Studies> Politics>Election: Running for 3rd grade class president Story	Literature> World classics: Stories of Sherlock Holmes Story	Literature> World classics: Adrift in the Pacific Story	
Book 10		Sports>Winter sports: Various aspects of some Winter Olympic sports Report				

* 10 books in each level will be published.

How to Use This Book

•Before Reading

You can easily find the topic and what kind of story you are about to read.

•The text

All the stories were written by professional writers from the U.S. and England, so you will read authentic and appropriate English sentences and expressions in every book in the series.

•Pop Quiz

Check out right away if you understand what you have just read by solving a pop quiz that checks your comprehension.

•Key Words

The key words and expressions on each page are listed for you to easily study them.

•Aha! Tips

Download free Korean explanations at *www.ihappyhouse.co.kr* for all of the sentences marked with "Aha!". These explain cultural, scientific, and economic knowledge or they deal with aspects of English such as grammatical structures or idiomatic expressions. There are lots of "Aha! Tips" to help you understand the text.

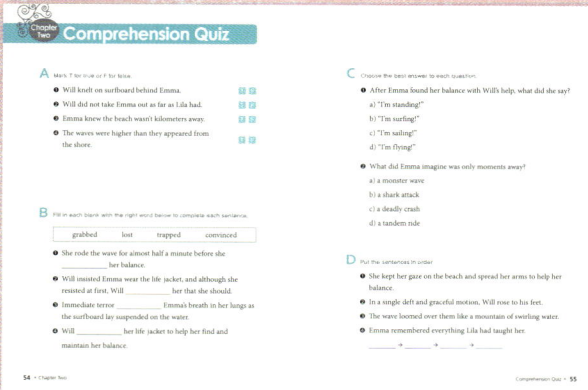

• Comprehension Quiz

After reading one chapter, solve various questions to find out if you fully understand the content.

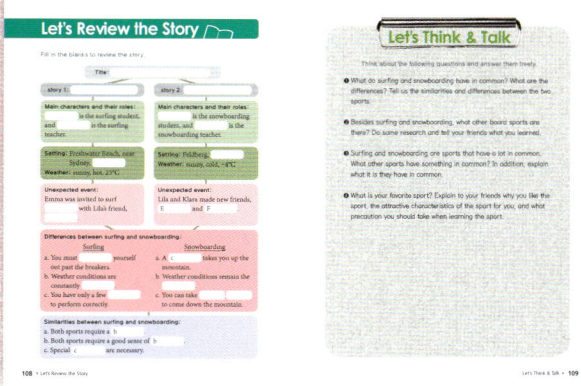

• Let's Review the Story /
• Let's Think & Talk

Fill in the blanks in the organizer to summarize the whole story. Express your own thinking and feelings about the story by answering the questions. You can build up logic and reasoning skills for your essay examinations in the future.

Appendix

Audio CD

In the CD audio book form, the texts are read vividly by American professional voice actors. (MP3 files downloaded for free)

After-reading Test

Solve an additionally provided After-reading Test for each book.

The Korean translation, Answer Keys, a Word Quiz, a Word List, and Aha! Tips for each book

You can download them for free at *www.ihappyhouse.co.kr* or *www.darakwon.co.kr*

Before Reading

Cool Board Sports

Level 6–5,
Lexile® 950L

• Sports > Board Sports
• Story

Dangerous yet exhilarating board sports

When you see surfers riding high waves wonderfully in the ocean, you are full of admiration for them. When surfing a surfer stands on a surfboard riding the waves washing ashore and performing wonderful moves while riding and shooting off of the waves. Not only is there the board sport of surfing at the beach, but there is also the board sport of snowboarding on a snow covered mountain. Snowboarding is a sport that applies surfing skills to skiing. The two sports have in common that people ride on boards and stand with one foot forward to keep their balance. In both sports, you feel exhilarated and excited when you almost fall down but manage not to. Which sport do you want to try? You will be fascinated by these cool board sports while reading the book.

Summary

Emma's family which lives in northern Australia visits their relatives in Sydney. During the visit, Emma learns how to surf from her cousin Lila. Lila teaches her how to lie down, stand up and keep her balance on a surfboard. After being taught how to do these things on the beach, Emma finally goes into the sea to surf. Will she be able to succeed?

During her vacation, Lila visits her friend Klara who lives in Germany. Klara teaches Lila how to snowboard on snow covered Feldberg, a mountain in the Black Forest. While learning how to snowboard, Lila finds out that snowboarding and surfing have a lot in common. Will Lila who is good at surfing also be attracted to snowboarding?

Let's read about these interesting trips together when one girl learn how to surf and another learns how to snowboard.

Contents

Cool Board Sports

✤ Even though the stories in the book take place in Australia and Germany, the speakers use American accents in the audio CD for learners' convenience.

Ride the Waves!

Chapter One

A Dream Come True

"Alec, guess what Mum just told me!" Thirteen-year-old Emma Smith called to her brother, ten-year-old Alec, from her seat across the aisle of the airplane taking them from Mount Isa in north-west Queensland to Sydney, Australia. "Cousin Lila is meeting us at Freshwater Beach, and she's going to teach me how to surf!"

Several years earlier, Lila had visited Emma and her family at their cattle station in the Northern Territory of Australia where they lived. Lila stayed for two weeks, and her myriad stories of surfers and surfing at Manly and Freshwater beaches had enthralled Emma. Emma thought Lila even looked like Sally Fitzgibbons, the famous Australian surfer, tall and willowy with a cascade of waist-length blonde tresses. And Emma knew Lila possessed the mandatory skills to teach her to surf, because Lila had promised to do just that should Emma ever visit Sydney, and now here she was!  Aha!

POP QUIZ

How did Emma feel about learning how to surf?

ⓐ She was excited about it.
ⓑ She didn't feel like it.

KEY WORDS

- a dream come true
  (cf. come true (come-came-come))
- call to
- seat
- aisle
- surf
- cattle station
- the Northern Territory (cf. northern / territory)

- myriad
- surfer
- enthrall
- willowy
- cascade
- tresses
- possess
- mandatory

Emma's excitement hummed through her body and made it difficult for her to sit still. The one thing Emma had always wanted to do was learn to surf, and now she would have the opportunity.

After the plane landed at the Sydney airport, the family collected their luggage, rented a car, and drove to the hotel where they would stay during their vacation. When they walked into the hotel lobby, Emma was the first to spy Lila, who stood waiting for them.

"Hello, there!" Lila squeezed Emma tightly. "It's so good to see you."

"Do you remember you said you would teach me how to surf?" Emma said without preamble, and her eagerness made Lila laugh.

Emma tossed and turned in her bed at the hotel that night, barely able to sleep or contain her burgeoning anticipation. Tomorrow would be the day she learned how to surf, and it would be a dream come true!

After breakfast the next morning, Lila arrived and helped the family gather everything they would need for a day at the beach: towels, a blanket, a cooler with food and drinks, beach toys, and sunscreen.

KEY WORDS

- excitement
- hum
- still
- opportunity
- land
- collect
- luggage

- spy
- squeeze
- without preamble
  (cf. preamble)
- eagerness
- toss and turn
- barely

- contain
- burgeoning
- anticipation
- gather
- cooler
- sunscreen

When they reached the parking lot, Emma's heart raced at the sight of two surfboards secured on the roof of Lila's vehicle, with one board being a bit shorter than the other. "Is the smaller board for me?" Emma asked, running up to the car. She laid her hand on the smooth surfboard. "Nope." Lila shook her head and her ponytail danced. "The longboard will be easier for you to learn on. It's wider than the shorter one, see?" Lila pointed at the longer surfboard.

"The longboard offers more stability and has a foam top instead of a fiberglass one, which is why it's the best choice when you're first starting out."

"How is the foam top helpful?" Emma said.

"It helps protect the people around you who might be hit by the board while you're learning, and the foam top also makes the board more buoyant."

"How long are the boards?" Alec wanted to know. He stood beside the car and eyed the surfboards with interest. "They both look pretty big to me."

"Emma's longboard is about 2.13 meters long, and my board is just shy of two meters."

POP QUIZ

Why was it best for Emma to learn surfing on a longboard?

ⓐ It offers better stability than shorter boards.
ⓑ It is made of lightweight plastic.

KEY WORDS

- reach
- parking lot
- race
- at the sight of
- surfboard
- secure
- a bit

- lay (lay-laid-laid)
- ponytail
- longboard
- point
- offer
- stability
- foam

- top
- fiberglass
- hit
- buoyant
- eye
- shy of

It was only a short drive to Freshwater Beach, but Emma couldn't contain her excitement. Today was the day she had dreamt of for so long. Today she would learn to surf! Together, they hauled everything from the car to the beach. Lila pointed out the restroom facilities and the lifeguard stations. She helped Mum and Dad find the best place to settle their belongings, and in spite of the crowd of people milling about on the beach, they located a comfortable spot near the water.

Emma hugged herself in an effort to contain her unbridled excitement. She breathed deeply. Oh, how she loved the scent of the sea! It differed so tremendously from the dry and dusty Outback, and although Emma loved her home in the Northern Territory, there was no denying she'd rather be at the beach. 📖 Aha!

KEY WORDS

- dream of
  (dream-dreamed/dreamt-dreamed/dreamt)
- haul
- point out
- facilities
- lifeguard
- station

- place
- settle
- belongings
- in spite of (= despite)
- a crowd of (cf. crowd)
- mill about
- locate
- spot

- effort
- unbridled
- scent
- tremendously
- dusty
- outback
- deny
- would rather (cf. rather)

The tang of salt water filled her nostrils and made them twitch. Over the sounds of children playing and people talking, waves crashed against the shore. Emma wriggled her toes and buried them in the sand with joy.

KEY WORDS

- tang
- salt water
- nostril

- twitch
- wave
- crash

- shore
- wriggle
- with joy

Emma scanned the water and waves. Surfers paddled their boards away from the beach beyond the breakers, and Emma knew they were preparing to catch a wave. Soon, she would join their ranks, and she, too, would stand on a surfboard and ride the waves. This was the best day ever!

"Look over there," Lila said to Emma and Alec. She pointed farther up the beach toward a headland. "Do you see that promontory jutting out into the water? There's a life-sized statue of Duke Kahanamoku built there, though we can't see it from here.  We'll walk over later in the week so you can see it."

"Who?" Alec wrinkled his nose, and Emma rolled her eyes at him.

"Duke Kahanamoku is only the most famous surfer of all time. He was born in Hawaii in 1890. He was an Olympic champion, and in 1914 he came here to Freshwater Beach and performed a surfing exhibition using a

▲ Duke Kahanamoku(1890~1968)

board he carved himself from local sugar pine. He did surfing tricks, too, including headstands! Some call him the father of modern surfing."

KEY WORDS

- scan
- paddle
- breaker
- rank
- headland
- promontory
- jut out into

- life-sized
- statue
- wrinkle
- roll one's eyes at
- of all time
- perform
- exhibition

- carve
- local
- sugar pine
- trick
- headstand

"That's right." Lila nodded and smiled. She was obviously impressed with Emma's knowledge of surfing history. "Most say Duke brought surfing to Australia, because its popularity began with his visit, but there were others who surfed here a few years before he did, like Tommy and William Walker, and a press clip shows Australia's first female surfer, Doris Stubbins, surfing as early as 1911. Still, Duke gets the credit for turning surfing into a favorite pastime for the Australians. His exhibition popularized the sport in Australia, and we've never looked back."

"I wish I could have been here that day. Maybe Duke Kahanamoku would have chosen me from the crowd instead of Isabel Letham." Emma sighed and stared off with a dreamy look in her eyes.

KEY WORDS

- nod
- obviously
- be impressed with
- knowledge
- popularity
- press
- clip
- get the credit for (get-got-gotten)
- turn A into B
- pastime

- Australian
- popularize
- never look back
- sigh
- stare off (cf. stare)
- dreamy
- look
- riding
- tandem
- confirmation

"The day of the exhibition, Duke chose a girl only a few years older than me from the crowd. He brought her into the water, helped her stand up when a wave came, and they surfed together on his board all the way back to the beach. That's called riding tandem, right?" Emma looked to Lila for confirmation.

POP QUIZ

Who was Australia's first female surfer?
ⓐ Doris Stubbins
ⓑ Isabel Letham

"That's right. No riding tandem for us, though," Lila said, and grinned at Emma. "The first thing I have to do is teach you to surf. Are you ready?"

Emma was so excited that all she could do was nod.

"First, lay your board in the sand, and I'll explain the different parts of the surfboard. The more pointed end of the board is the nose, and the rear is called the tail. The rails are the edges of the surfboard, and they run from the tail to the nose. The deck is the whole top of the board.

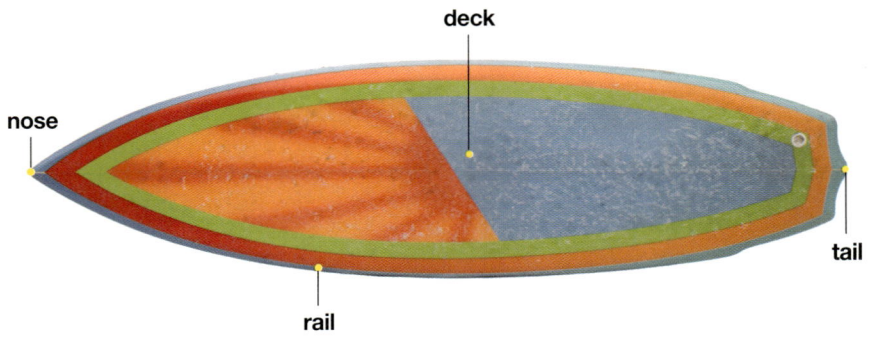

▲ leash

The cord attached to the tail is called a leash, and you'll attach this to your ankle to prevent you from losing your board when you wipe out. 🌐 Any questions?" Lila asked, and Emma shook her head.

"You're wearing your rash guard. That's good."
"The rash guard will protect my upper body from abrasions caused by sand and rocks, right?" said Emma. "And from sunburn."

▲ rash guard

KEY WORDS

- grin at
- pointed
- rear
- edge
- cord

- attach
- leash
- prevent A from + *Verb*-ing
- wipe out
- rash guard

- upper body
- abrasion
- sunburn

"Absolutely," Lila nodded. "Okay, now, before learning to stand up on the surfboard you must practice riding the waves lying down, as this will help you practice the body movement. Let's try it here on the sand first. Lay down on the board on your stomach. 📖 Scoot back so your toes are touching the board's tail. Begin in this position, understanding that once you're in the water, if you're too far forward, you might nosedive. If you're back too far, the wave will go under the board. With practice, you'll learn the exact placement of your weight on the board. But for now, begin with your feet touching the tail. Grab the rails of the board at the level of your chest with your elbows poking out in a posture sort of like chicken wings."

Emma laughed at Lila's description, but did as she was told.

KEY WORDS

- absolutely
- scoot
- position
- understand
  (understand-understood-understood)
- forward
- nosedive
- placement
- for now
- grab

- level
- chest
- poke out
- posture
- description
- bent
- back and forth
- keep one's eyes on
- want
- head

"Is this correct?" Emma asked, moving her bent elbows back and forth.

"Perfect. Now raise up your chin and chest, and look out over the nose. When you surf, you'll keep your eyes on the beach — you want to look toward where you're headed, not where you are."

Emma practiced laying down on the board, positioning her arms and hands, and lifting up her chin and chest. When she felt confident, Lila brought her into the water.

"Put your board in the water and push it out as you wade to about waist deep, and jump over oncoming waves to let them pass. Watch for waves that are coming in straight toward the beach, as those will be the easiest for you to ride. 📖 When you see one coming, lie on your board, lift up your chin and chest as you practiced, and ride the wave back to the beach!" Emma followed Lila's instructions and did everything just as she had practiced. She loved the powerful rush of the waves beneath her, catapulting her toward the sandy beach, and she was glad to be wearing her rash guard for those times she tumbled from the board.

KEY WORDS

- lift
- confident
- wade
- oncoming
- watch for
- straight
- lie (lie-lay-lain)
- instruction
- rush
- catapult
- tumble

POP QUIZ

Why did Lila tell Emma to watch for waves coming in straight toward the beach?

ⓐ They are slower moving than other waves.
ⓑ They are easier to ride.

After about thirty minutes or so, Lila brought Emma back to the sand for another lesson.

"Run hard and skid in the sand so we can see which foot you put in front of you," Lila said.

Emma shook her head because Lila's request sounded silly, but she did as asked and discovered that she put her left foot forward when she skidded to a stop.

▲ regular surfer

▲ goofy surfer

"You pushed your left foot in front of you, and that means you're a *regular* surfer. Had you put your right foot in front of you, you'd be a *goofy* surfer," Lila said. 🌐 "But we now know that your left foot will be in front of you while you're surfing."

"I'm glad I'm not goofy," Emma said, laughing, and Lila laughed too.

POP QUIZ

Which type of stance did Emma have while surfing?

ⓐ goofy   ⓑ regular

KEY WORDS

- skid
- request

- silly
- regular

- goofy

"Being a goofy surfer isn't wrong; it's just the name it was given," Lila said. "Lay the board down in the sand and lie face down as before, turning your right foot so that the inside of your ankle is touching the deck. Lift your chin and chest, and slide your other foot forward to your chest line, then let go of the board and stand up. Use your shoulders and arms to help you balance, and bend your legs at the knees to put a bit of weight on the front leg. And remember, you keep your gaze on the beach as you ride in." Lila grinned. "That's all there is to it. Practice on your board here in the sand, and then we'll head into the water and you can give it a go!"

Emma practiced until her movements were easy and sure, and she called to Lila when she was ready to try standing on her board in the water for the first time. Lila, who had been talking to Emma's mother, jogged over to Emma.

▲ wipeout
(a surfer falling off his or her board accidentally because of high waves or doing so on purpose)

"One last thing you have to know," Lila said, "is how to wipe out in a way that will help you prevent an injury. Wiping out is part of surfing, and you can't just dive off the board. When a wipeout happens, you'll take a deep breath and fall backwards off the surfboard, wrapping your arms around your head to protect it. Got it?"

"Got it." Emma nodded. She felt certain she knew what to do. "Let's catch a wave, then, shall we?"

KEY WORDS

- face
- **slide** (slide-slid-slid/slidden)
- let go of
- **bend** (bend-bent-bent)
- gaze
- **That's all there is to it.** (= That's all. / That's it.)
- **give it a go** (= give it a try[shot])
  (give-gave-given)
- for the first time

- jog
- wipe out
- injury
- **dive off** (dive-dived/dove-dived)
- wipeout
- **take a deep breath** (take-took-taken)
- backwards
- wrap

A Mark T for true or F for false.

❶ Duke Kahanamoku is the most famous surfer of all time. T F

❷ Duke Kahanamoku was born in Hawaii. T F

❸ Duke Kahanamoku was an Olympic champion. T F

❹ Duke Kahanamoku rode tandem with Sally Fitzgibbons. T F

B Fill in each blank with the right word below to complete each sentence.

secured	turned	lobby	raced
excitement	spy	tossed	still

❶ Emma's _____ hummed through her body and made it
difficult for her to sit _____.

❷ When they walked into the hotel _____, Emma was
the first to _____ Lila.

❸ Emma _____ and _____ in her bed at the
hotel that night.

❹ Emma's heart _____ at the sight of two surfboards
_____ on the roof of Lila's vehicle.

C Choose the best answer to each question.

❶ What are two of the benefits to having a foam top longboard?

a) weight and protection for those who may be hit with the board

b) buoyancy and weight

c) buoyancy and protection for those who may be hit with the board

d) weight and width

❷ What did Lila ask Emma to do that Emma thought was silly?

a) position her arms and legs

b) run hard and skid in the sand

c) practice in the sand

d) ride a wave back to the beach

D Put the sentences in order.

❶ Scoot back so your toes are touching the board's tail.

❷ Grab the rails of the board at the level of your chest with your elbows poking.

❸ Raise up your chin and chest, and look out over the nose.

❹ Lay down on the board on your stomach.

_____ → _____ → _____ → _____

Surfing Surprise

Emma grabbed her surfboard and followed Lila into the water. She pushed the surfboard out as she waded and stopped with Lila when they were waist deep.

Lila taught Emma how to wait for the right wave — in this case, a wave that was coming in straight and headed directly for the beach. Emma suffered many false starts and wipeouts, and frustration oozed through her.

"Don't give up," Lila told her. "You can do this, Emma."

Emma waited for the next wave. She turned her board and dove onto it, careful to position her hands and feet as she had practiced. She pulled her forward foot to her chest, let go of the board and stood up, bending at the knees and using her arms for balance.

KEY WORDS

- surprise
- directly
- suffer
- false

- frustration
- ooze
- give up
- pull

- suck in
- clap
- whoop

This time, she didn't fall off the surfboard! She rode the wave for almost half a minute before she lost her balance and had to suck in a deep breath, cover her head, and fall backwards. Lila and the rest of Emma's family stood on the beach watching her, jumping and clapping.

"Whoop, whoop! You did it, Emma!" Alec cried, dancing in the sand.

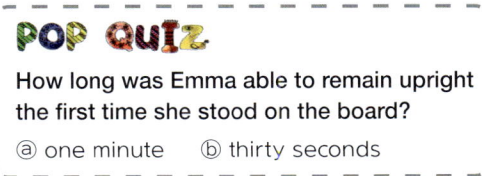

POP QUIZ

How long was Emma able to remain upright the first time she stood on the board?

ⓐ one minute   ⓑ thirty seconds

Emma waved to her family, and Lila left them to meet Emma at the water's edge.

"That was amazing!" Emma said. Adrenaline pumped through her blood making it difficult for her to stand still. "I couldn't stay up for long, but I know I'll get better with practice. I'm a surfer! Thank you so much, Lila, for teaching me!"

"You're welcome! You're improving so fast; it's clear you have a talent for surfing. And I've got a surprise for you," Lila said.

"Do you see that guy with the blond hair jogging toward us? He's wearing the red boardies."

Emma understood that boardies was the slang term for board shorts, or swim shorts. She squinted her eyes against the glare of the sun, scanned the beach for the person Lila had pointed out, and identified him when he waved at Lila. Lila smiled and waved back with enthusiasm.

POP QUIZ

What are "boardies"?

ⓐ special lifesaving vests worn by surfers
ⓑ the slang term for swim shorts or board shorts

KEY WORDS

- water's edge
- Adrenaline
- pump
- improve

- have a talent for
- slang
- term
- board shorts

- squint
- glare
- identify
- enthusiasm

"This is my friend, Will," Lila said after Will reached them.
"Hello, there," Will said. "Emma, right? Nice to meet you."
"Will is one of my surfing instructors, and he does
competitive surfing." Lila said. "He has also played the
part of Duke Kahanamoku in a few reenactments here on the
beach over the last few years."

"I don't understand." Emma drew her brows together in confusion.

"Remember the story you told Alec about Isabel Letham, the fifteen-year-old girl Duke Kahanamoku chose from the crowd to do a tandem surf with him during his exhibition here in 1914? Will has playacted the part of Duke for several reenactments, complete with the fancy headstands and other surfing tricks."

POP QUIZ

Which famous surfer did Will play the part of for reenactments?

ⓐ Duke Kahanamoku
ⓑ Isabel Letham

KEY WORDS

- instructor
- competitive
- reenactment
- draw one's brows together (draw-drew-drawn)

- in confusion
- playact
- complete with
- fancy

"The surfing club to which I belong sponsors a demonstration show for visitors every year," Will explained. "We reenact Duke's exhibition for spectators here at Freshwater Beach."

"Oh!" Emma laughed and nodded. "Okay. Now I understand."

"We have a reenactment scheduled soon, and Lila suggested that you might like to help me practice. How do you feel about participating in tandem surfing?" Will asked. "We'll practice just the way I'll do it for the show."

Emma stared in surprise at Will and her heart raced with excitement. She turned her wide eyes toward Lila, who laughed and drew Emma into a fond embrace.

POP QUIZ

How did Emma feel about participating in tandem surfing?

ⓐ She felt excited.

ⓑ She felt annoyed.

KEY WORDS

- belong to
- sponsor
- demonstration
- reenact

- spectator (= audience)
- scheduled
- suggest
- participate in

- fond
- embrace

"Get ready, Emma, because you're about to ride a monster wave with one of the premier surfers in all of Australia!" Lila said.

Emma waited while Will disappeared up the beach after promising to return momentarily. When he came back, he carried a life jacket and a surfboard, and the board was a meter longer than the one Emma had borrowed from Lila. Will insisted Emma wear the life jacket, and although she resisted at first, Will convinced her that she should.

"Lila said you're a strong and competent swimmer," Will told her, "but the vest will help ensure your safety. You ready to surf?"

Too excited to speak, all Emma could do was nod.

"Let's go then," Will said.

Will knelt on the surfboard behind Emma and together they paddled out through the breakers.

Emma's anticipation increased when they skimmed the surfboard farther than Emma had dared to go while surfing with Lila.

KEY WORDS

- disappear (↔ appear)
- momentarily
- life jacket
- borrow
- insist
- resist
- at first
- convince
- competent

- ensure
- safety
- kneel (kneel-kneeled/knelt-kneeled/knelt)
- increase
- skim
- dare to + *Verb*
- glance at
- perspective
- observe

Emma glanced at the shore behind them, and from her perspective the beach appeared to be kilometers away, though Emma knew that wasn't true.

Still, they had paddled out past the breakers now, and the waves rose higher than they appeared when observing them while standing on the shore.

"Do we have to worry about sharks out here?" Emma asked, glancing around fearfully. "Mick Fanning was attacked by a great white shark in a surfing competition not long ago." "Mick was surfing in South Africa when the shark attacked him, not here at Freshwater Beach. I'd be lying if I said we've never seen sharks here. Sharks live in the ocean, and that means surfers run the risk of encountering them, so while it's best to stay vigilant, you can't let that fear overcome your desire to surf. For right now, I don't see any giant fins skimming the water, do you?" Will said.

"No," Emma said.

"At the moment, I'm less concerned about sharks and more concerned about waiting for the perfect wave for us to surf," Will said, his eyes watching the horizon. "When our wave comes, I'll turn the board around and stand up, and you need to stand up when I do, okay?"

"What if I fall?" Emma asked, excitement and fear warring inside her.

"The vest will provide protection for you and allow you to remain afloat should you require it, but try not to think or worry about the prospect of falling. I'll hold onto you the whole time we're surfing, and we're going to cruise right up to the beach." He nodded toward an oncoming wave. "This is the one we've been waiting for, Emma, so be prepared!"

KEY WORDS

- fearfully
- great white shark
- competition
- run the risk of
- encounter
- vigilant
- overcome (overcome-overcame-overcome)
- desire
- fin
- at the moment
- be concerned about
- horizon
- What if ~?
- war
- protection
- allow
- remain
- afloat
- require
- prospect
- hold onto
- cruise

The wave loomed over them like a mountain of swirling
water, bigger than any Emma had seen, and she swallowed
a frightened scream when Will spun the surfboard around to
face the shore, putting the wave at their backs.
Immediate terror trapped Emma's breath in her lungs as the
surfboard lay suspended on the water.

In a single deft and graceful motion, Will rose to his feet, grabbed Emma by the life jacket and tugged it in an attempt to raise her up from her knees. "This is your moment, Emma. Stand up."

Emma took a deep breath and remembered everything Lila had taught her. She stood up on the surfboard, and Will grabbed her life jacket to help her find and maintain her balance.

KEY WORDS

- loom over
- a mountain of
- swirling
- swallow
- frightened
- scream
- **spin** (spin-spun-spun)

- immediate
- terror
- trap
- lung
- suspend
- deft
- graceful

- motion
- rise to one's feet
  (rise-rose-risen)
- tug
- attempt
- maintain

A moment later the surfboard became elevated upon the crest of the wave, teetering there, and Emma's stomach lurched and seemed to bounce into her throat and then drop like a stone against her ribs. She imagined this must be exactly what falling off a cliff would be like, with a deadly crash only moments away!

Fear swam inside of her, but she kept her gaze on the beach and spread out her arms to help her balance.

"Look at you, surfer girl!" Will shouted. "You're a natural!" Emma sucked in a breath and allowed herself to experience the thrill of viewing the world from this unique perspective. She was surfing a big wave in tandem with a professional surfer, and he had called her a natural!

I'm flying! Emma thought as the wind whipped her short hair about her face and salty sea spray tingled against her skin.

POP QUIZ

How did Emma feel while riding in tandem with Will?
ⓐ like she was flying
ⓑ like she was dancing

KEY WORDS

- elevated
- crest
- teeter
- lurch
- bounce
- rib
- cliff

- deadly
- only moments away
- swim (swim-swam-swum)
- Look at you!
- natural
- allow oneself to[in]
- thrill

- view
- unique
- whip
- sea spray
- tingle

Her trepidation fled, crushed by enthusiasm and replaced with soaring joy.

"I'm flying!" She cried out, laughing.

The wave's eventual denouement came too soon for Emma. It led to a breathtaking crash of water and spray, and brought the surfboard nearer the shore.

Emma kept her eyes open against the splash of water and sea spray, refusing to miss even a single moment of this tandem ride. Will maneuvered the board so that they rode it, still standing, right onto the beach.

"Way to go, Emma!" Emma's family cheered for her. Aha!

"I'm hooked for life!" Emma exclaimed, her eyes shining with exhilaration and joy. She threw her arms wide and spun in a gleeful pirouette right there in the sand.

"You know," Lila said, "that's precisely what Isabel Letham said after riding tandem with Duke Kahanamoku."

KEY WORDS

- trepidation
- flee (flee-fled-fled)
- replace A with B
- soaring
- eventual
- denouement
- lead (lead-led-led)
- breathtaking
- splash

- maneuver
- cheer for
- be hooked
- for life
- exclaim
- exhilaration
- gleeful
- pirouette
- precisely

"That's right, it is," Emma said. "I can't wait to be back in the water. Now that I've surfed by myself and with Will, and I know how wonderful it feels to ride a wave, all I want to do is keep surfing!"

KEY WORDS

- now that   · by oneself (= alone)

"I'd like to see someone try and stop us." Lila captured Emma by the hand and together they ran toward the place where their surfboards lay waiting in the sand.

"Will has already paddled out past the breakers," Emma said to Lila, and pointed to where Will was standing waist deep in water and surveying the waves.

"Look how far he goes. He's awesome, and that tandem ride was the best surprise I've ever had. Aha! I really have a feel for it now."

"I knew you'd be thrilled," Lila said. "And you were awesome out there."

POP QUIZ

What did Emma say was the best surprise she had ever had?

ⓐ tandem ride
ⓑ learning to surf

KEY WORDS

- capture
- by the hand
- survey

- have a feel for
- thrilled
- awesome

- sparkle
- match

"There's only one thing more to say before we hit the water,"
Emma said.

"Oh? What's that?" Lila asked.

The happy sparkle in Emma's eyes was matched by the joy
in her voice when she smiled wide and said, "It's time to
catch a wave!"

Comprehension Quiz

A Mark T for true or F for false.

❶ Will knelt on surfboard behind Emma.　　　　　　T　F

❷ Will did not take Emma out as far as Lila had.　　T　F

❸ Emma knew the beach wasn't kilometers away.　　T　F

❹ The waves were higher than they appeared from
the shore.　　　　　　　　　　　　　　　　　　T　F

B Fill in each blank with the right word below to complete each sentence.

grabbed	lost	trapped	convinced

❶ She rode the wave for almost half a minute before she

_____ her balance.

❷ Will insisted Emma wear the life jacket, and although she

resisted at first, Will _____ her that she should.

❸ Immediate terror _____ Emma's breath in her lungs as

the surfboard lay suspended on the water.

❹ Will _____ her life jacket to help her find and

maintain her balance.

C

Choose the best answer to each question.

❶ After Emma found her balance with Will's help, what did she say?

a) "I'm standing!"

b) "I'm surfing!"

c) "I'm sailing!"

d) "I'm flying!"

❷ What did Emma imagine was only moments away?

a) a monster wave

b) a shark attack

c) a deadly crash

d) a tandem ride

D

Put the sentences in order.

❶ She kept her gaze on the beach and spread her arms to help her balance.

❷ In a single deft and graceful motion, Will rose to his feet.

❸ The wave loomed over them like a mountain of swirling water.

❹ Emma remembered everything Lila had taught her.

_____ → _____ → _____ → _____

Fly on the Snow!

Chapter One

Friends in Feldberg

Lila Smith stood in the snow with her gloved hands resting on her hips, a wool hat pulled over her ears, and a smile on her face.

Lila's friend, Klara Reinhart, regarded her with an answering smile. "So what do you think of Feldberg?" Klara asked, spreading her arms wide.

"Beautiful," Lila said, gazing at the snowcapped pines.

"I knew it would be, of course, being in the Black Forest Mountains of Germany, but I never expected it to be this amazing. You know what else is amazing? That just a week ago I was teaching my cousin, Emma, to surf on Freshwater Beach. I feel as if I've crossed into a different world."

"Germany is a long way from Australia, that's for sure," Klara said. "And in another couple of hours you'll receive your first snowboarding lesson. Although I love those Ugg boots you're wearing, you'll have to trade them for ski boots before we head to the slopes."

"I know." Lila sighed. "I hate to take them off, though. I love my Uggs!"

POP QUIZ

Feldberg is located in the Black Forest Mountains of _____.

ⓐ Germany
ⓑ Australia

KEY WORDS

- Feldberg
- gloved
- rest on
- hip
- regard
- answering

- snowcapped
- pine
- Black Forest
- as if
- for sure (= certainly)
- snowboarding

- Ugg boot
- trade A for B
- slope
- take off

"Did you pack everything I suggested you would need?"
Klara asked.

"You supplied me with a list of items that are necessary for
snowboarding, and I'm quite certain I have everything," Lila
assured Klara. "I've brought boots, a beanie and protective
helmet, goggles, a jacket, a vest, and gloves, all designed for
snowboarding."

Lila regarded her friend with a bemused smile. "All I need for surfing is my board, a leash, and a rash guard or wetsuit. Compared to surfing, snowboarding requires so much gear!"

"Did you remember what I told you about layering your clothes? Did you bring sufficient attire?" Klara asked.

"Of course." Lila gave Klara a teasing shove. "I've got my base layer — snowboarding socks, a thermal body shirt —" Lila dropped her voice to a whisper, "— and thermal underwear."

"You don't have to whisper," Klara said, laughing, and her warm breath collided with the cold air and created puffs of white.

KEY WORDS

- pack
- supply A with B
- assure
- beanie
- goggles
- bemused
- wetsuit
- compared to

- gear
- layer
- sufficient
- attire
- give a shove
- teasing
- base
- thermal

- body shirt
- drop one's voice
- whisper
- underwear
- collide with
- create
- puff

"Around here there's nothing unusual about wearing thermal underwear this time of year. In fact, you need to wear it on the slopes. January is our coldest month, and it's −4 degrees Celsius at the base of the mountain today."

"Don't remind me," Lila shivered. "Only a week ago I was standing on Freshwater Beach enjoying the sunshine in my bikini, and it was 23 degrees Celsius."

She shivered again and tucked her gloved hands inside the pockets of her wool coat.

"Let's go inside," Klara said, "and then we'll head to the slopes for your first snowboarding lesson."

POP QUIZ

What is the coldest month in Feldberg?

ⓐ February
ⓑ January

KEY WORDS

- unusual
- degree
- Celsius
- remind
- shiver

- bikini
- tuck
- rent
- run one's fingers through hair
- cap

- braid
- with envy
- as long as
- matter

Lila followed her friend into the hotel where Klara's family
had rented rooms for the weekend. Both girls removed their
gloves and hats. Klara ran her fingers through her short cap
of dark hair and Lila, who wore her own long hair in a thick
braid, watched her friend with envy.

"I love your short hair," she said to Klara. "I'm not brave
enough to cut mine off."

"As long as you're brave on the ski slopes, that's all that
matters," Klara said.

"I'm glad you decided to accept our invitation to join us
on this vacation. I'd love for you to visit us at our home in
Berlin some time, too, but when my mother said I could
invite a friend on this Feldberg ski trip, I knew I wanted it to
be you."

"I'm delighted you invited me, Klara. I'm so happy to be
here." Lila opened her arms and drew Klara into a warm
hug.

The girls became best friends during Klara's stay as an exchange student at Lila's school in Sydney, Australia. Klara had returned home to Germany after a year, but she and Lila stayed in contact and remained the dearest of friends.

"Lunch first," Klara said, "and then we'll change clothes, hit the slopes, and I'll teach you how to snowboard. I want you to love snowboarding as much as you love surfing."

POP QUIZ

How did Lila and Klara first meet?

ⓐ Lila was an Australian exchange student in Germany.

ⓑ Klara was a German exchange student in Australia.

▲ Feldberg

KEY WORDS

- decide
- accept
- invitation

- delighted
- exchange student
- stay in contact

- dearest

After lunch, the girls went to their hotel room and changed into their snowboarding gear. This consisted of long thermal undergarments and socks as a base layer, and a second layer comprised of a fleece jacket and thermal pants.

Over this they each wore an outer layer of a jacket and pants that were waterproof, windproof, and designed to allow perspiration to escape while shielding the body from the elements. Lila also wore a vest over her outer layer as she wasn't accustomed to the cold.

And of course, they wore their snowboarding boots, helmets, and gloves, and carried their goggles with them. Lila didn't own a snowboard, so Klara had brought one for her to use.

POP QUIZ

How many layers of clothes did Lila wear for snowboarding?

ⓐ three
ⓑ four

KEY WORDS

- consist of
- undergarment
- comprised of
- fleece
- outer
- waterproof
- windproof

- perspiration
- escape
- shield A from B (*cf.* shield)
- elements
- be accustomed to
- load
- sport utility vehicle(SUV)

- accessibility
- ski lift
- chat to
- direct
- attention

Klara's father loaded the snowboards into the back of his sport utility vehicle. Feldberg offered easy accessibility to the ski lifts by car, and while Klara's parents chatted to each other in German, a language Lila didn't understand, Klara directed Lila's attention to things outside the window as they drove.

"Feldberg is the highest mountain in Germany outside of the Alps, but it is still a low mountain range by comparison, not quite 1,500 meters," Klara said.

"How much taller are the Bavarian Alps?" Lila asked.

"Well, Zugspitze is just shy of 3,000 meters, almost twice as tall as Feldberg. 🌐 But Feldberg is a wonderful ski resort, has perfect slopes for beginning skiers and snowboarders, as you will soon discover, as well as," Klara glanced at her parents and dropped her voice to a whisper, "cute boys!"

Lila widened her eyes and laughed, and Klara joined in and laughed too.

"I think I'll worry about the snowboarding first," Lila said. "Do you think I'll be able to do any real snowboarding today? Is it hard to learn?"

"I think surfing is harder," Klara responded. "But you taught me to surf in one afternoon last year at Freshwater Beach, so I'm taking that as a challenge to teach you to snowboard in one afternoon, as well. Because you are an accomplished surfer, I believe you will discover snowboarding to be a complimentary sport in some ways."

POP QUIZ

Which did Klara think was harder to learn?
ⓐ snowboarding
ⓑ surfing

KEY WORDS

- outside of
- the Alps
- mountain range
- by comparison
- not quite
- Bavarian

- Zugspitze
- skier
- snowboarder
- as well as
- widen
- respond

- challenge
- as well
- accomplished
- complimentary
- in some ways

There was only a small line of vehicles waiting to pull into the parking lot near the ski lifts, and it wasn't long before Herr Reinhart, Klara's father, had parked the SUV and removed the snowboards from the rear of the vehicle.  Aha! He removed skis for himself and Frau Reinhart, Klara's mother, and they waved goodbye to the girls with an agreement to meet them at the base lodge in a few hours.

"Viel Glück!" Herr Reinhart called as he and Frau Reinhart headed toward the ski lifts. "Good luck!"

"So what do we do first?" Lila asked Klara. "I'm ready to snowboard."

"Good!" Klara said. "I'm going ask some questions and tell you to do some things that may sound familiar." She smiled at Lila. "So, do you ride regular or goofy?"

"Seriously?" Lila laughed. "That's just like surfing. You know I ride regular, with my left foot leading."

POP QUIZ

What two terms are the same in snowboarding and surfing?

ⓐ goofy and regular

ⓑ skating and sliding

KEY WORDS

- pull into
- it wan't long before ~
- Herr (= Mr.)
- remove A from B
- Frau (= Mrs. / Madam)
- agreement
- lodge
- Viel Glück!
- familiar

"Exactly. Snowboarding uses those same terms. The first thing I'm going to teach you is skating, or one-footed riding, because that's how you'll get around on the slope and get to and from the ski lift. We'll practice right here where the ground is level. Place your lead foot in the front binding and strap up." Klara watched Lila strap into her binding, and then she strapped into hers.

"Now you'll practice sliding forward, using your free foot to push off, kind of like the way you skateboard. As with surfing, you want to look ahead toward where you're going." 📖
Aha!

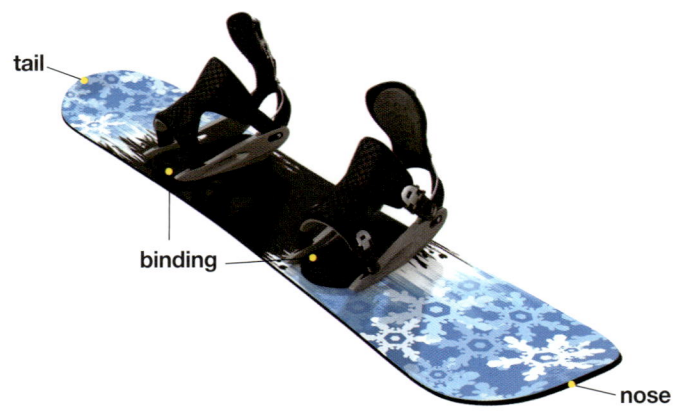

tail

binding

nose

KEY WORDS

- one-footed
- get around
- lead foot
- binding

- strap
- kind of like (= similarly)
- demonstrate
- copy

- proceed
- with caution

Klara demonstrated the motion and then waited while Lila copied her movements. Klara slid fast on her snowboard, but Lila proceeded with caution until she learned the feel of sliding on the snow.

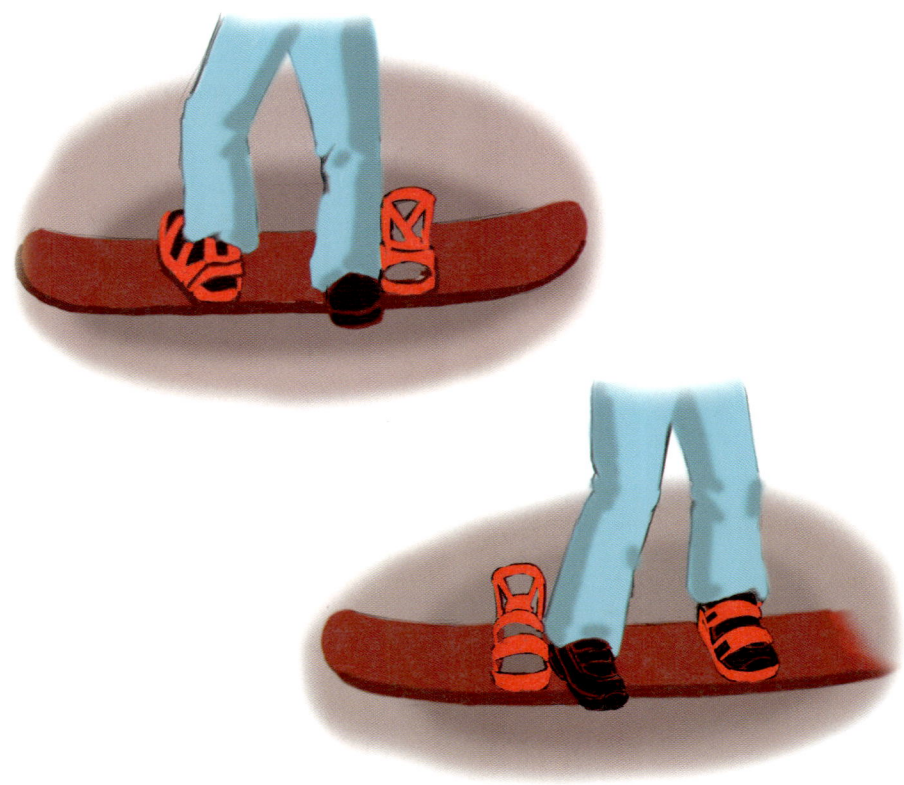

"The next step is to push off with your free foot, but then rest your free foot on the board, between the bindings. To stop, you'll move your free foot to the back edge of the board and drag your heel in the snow, or to the front edge of the board and drag your toes in the snow, whichever method you find to be the most comfortable."

Lila and Klara practiced skating on level ground, as Klara had promised, before finding an area that sloped gently.

Lila wasn't sure she liked the sensation of having her lead foot attached to the board, as this was clumsy and quite different from surfing, but with time and repetition her movements became more natural and fluid.

"Now that you've learned to skate, you're ready for the ski lift." Klara said. "The first time on and off can be a little tricky, but I'll help you, and after we're at the top of the run I'll show you how to strap into both bindings, and how to stand up. After that we'll get into more of the basics of snowboarding and you can practice going downhill."

POP QUIZ

Where did Lila and Klara practice skating?

ⓐ on level ground
ⓑ on a gentle slope

KEY WORDS

- drag
- heel
- whichever
- method
- comfortable

- gently
- sensation
- clumsy
- with time
- repetition

- fluid
- tricky
- run
- basics
- downhill

 A Mark T for true or F for false.

❶ Klara's home was in Berlin. ☐T ☐F

❷ Lila was a visiting exchange student. ☐T ☐F

❸ Lila was visiting on vacation. ☐T ☐F

❹ Klara and Lila had been friends since they were infants. ☐T ☐F

B Choose the best answer to each question.

❶ What was the first thing Klara wanted to teach Lila?

a) one-footed riding (skating)

b) how not to layer her clothing

c) how to slow down

d) how to ride the ski lift

❷ Klara's parents agreed to meet the girls in a few hours. Where were they to meet?

a) at the ski lift

b) at the base lodge

c) at the top of the slope

d) at the car

C Solve the crossword puzzle.

❷ left-foot leading

❹ A base _____ is comprised of long thermal undergarments and socks.

❺ one-footed sliding

Down

❶ _____ foot is not strapped into bindings while you skate.

❸ worn for eye protection while snowboarding

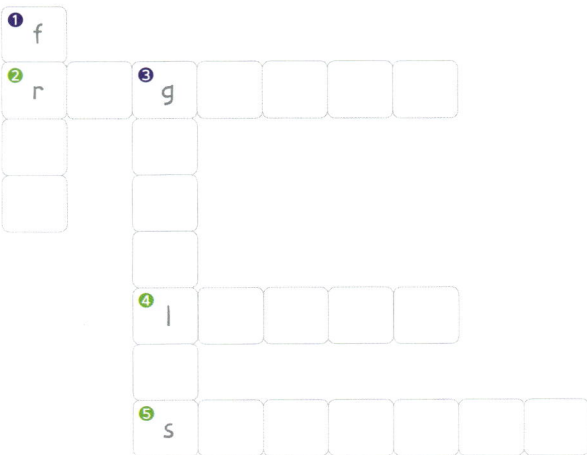

Chapter Two

Friendly Foursome

They skated to the ski lift and, while they waited for their turn to sit down on a chair, Lila noticed two boys standing in line behind her and Klara. She thought they looked like salt and pepper — one blond and one dark-haired, just like Lila and Klara.

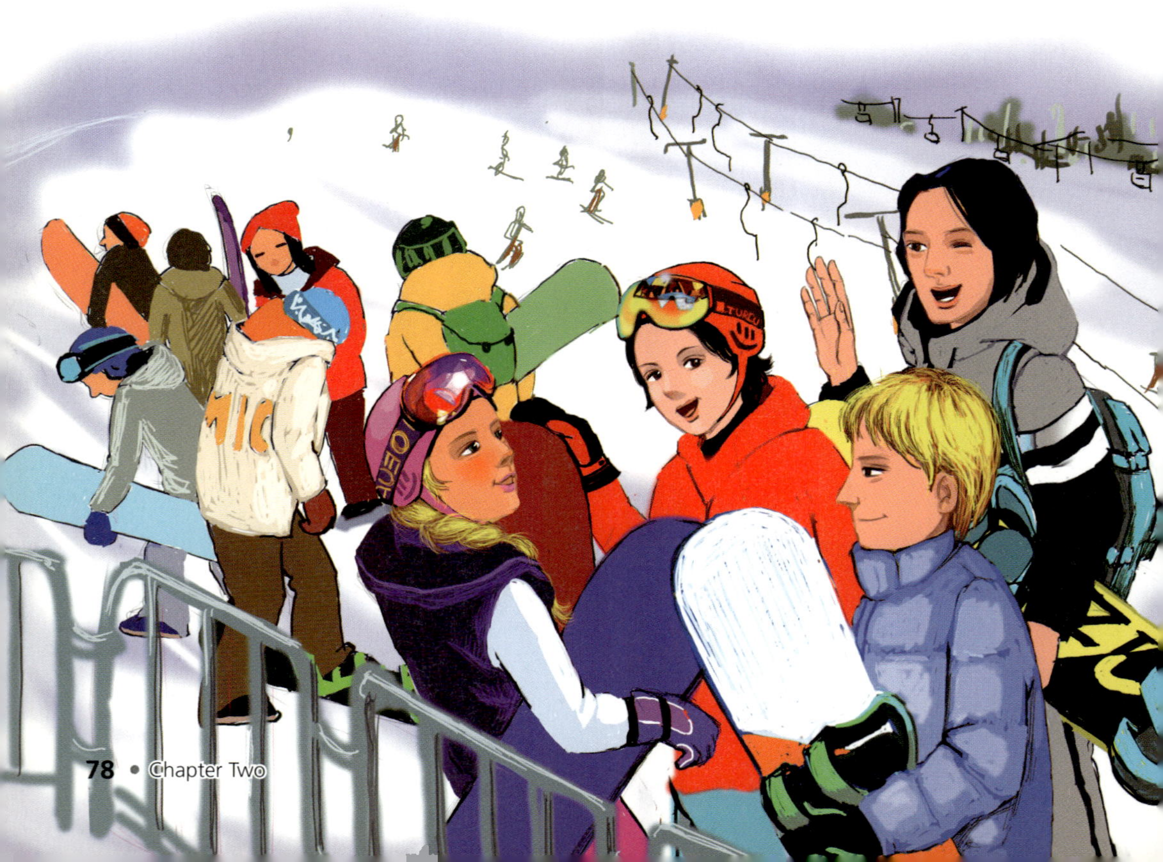

The dark-haired boy smiled and waved at Lila. Lila's cheeks heated up and she hoped he couldn't see her blushing. She averted her eyes quickly and focused on what Klara was telling her about the ski lift. Klara explained to Lila that the lift would glide up behind them and they would simply sit down, as if someone were holding a chair for them in a restaurant.

The boy who had smiled and waved at Lila called out something in German which Lila didn't understand.

She looked askance at Klara who chuckled. "It appears you have an admirer. He said he'd be happy to hold a chair for you anytime."

POP QUIZ

Why did Lila compare the two boys to salt and pepper?

ⓐ They were always together.
ⓑ One was blond and the other was dark-haired.

KEY WORDS

- foursome
- notice
- stand in line
- dark-haired

- heat up
- blush
- avert
- focus on

- glide
- look askance at
- chuckle
- admirer

Lila's cheeks grew warm again, and when the chair glided up behind her, it caught her by surprise and she dropped onto the seat with a gasp.

Klara lowered the safety bar and the chair began its ascent up the mountain, carried by a circulating rope cable.

"When it's time to get off the lift, stand up with your free foot against the binding. Keep your knees bent a little while you slide, and drag your toes or heel to come to a stop," Klara said.

Lila nodded at Klara's instructions, but her attention was on the view. Without a cloud in sight, the cerulean sky seemed to stretch forever, pierced by the tips of the towering pines that grew on the mountainside.

KEY WORDS

- catch ~ by surprise (catch-caught-caught)
- gasp
- lower
- ascent
- circulating
- come to a stop
- in sight
- cerulean
- stretch
- pierce
- tip
- towering
- mountainside
- bathe
- (be) strewn with (strew-strewed-strewed/strewn)
- marvel at
- surround
- tremble

Sunshine bathed the hills, the snow sparkled as if strewn with diamonds, and Lila marveled at the beauty surrounding her. She shivered, but not from the cold. It was excitement that caused her to tremble.

POP QUIZ

What was it that caused Lila to tremble?

ⓐ the cold
ⓑ excitement

"Remember now," Klara said as their lift neared the tier
where they would climb off, "free foot against the binding,
knees bent, and drag to stop. Don't be nervous, because I'm
right here with you."

Getting off the chairlift with one foot attached to the
snowboard was harder than Lila thought it would be, and
she almost fell over when her board hit the snow and began
to slide.

"Drag to stop," Klara reminded her, and though Lila wobbled a bit, she didn't fall down, and managed to bring herself to a stop.

"Nice job!" Klara said. "Now let me teach you how to strap up both feet and stand up."

Lila copied Klara and laid her snowboard upside down so the bindings were in the snow, and it was apparent to her that this prevented the board from sliding away. Aha!

Next, the girls sat down in the snow, bent their knees, and strapped both feet into the bindings.

POP QUIZ
What are the steps Klara gave Lila for getting off the ski lift?
ⓐ Jump off, knees bent, and drag to stop.
ⓑ Free foot against the binding, knees bent, and drag to stop.

KEY WORDS

- tier
- climb off (= get off)
- chairlift
- fall over (fall-fell-fallen)
- wobble

- fall down
- manage
- upside down
- apparent (= obvious)

"To stand," Klara said, "reach forward and grab the edge of the board. Use that hand to pull yourself up while you use the other hand to push yourself up. See?"

Klara enacted the movements with ease, and Lila copied her, but with little success.

"It's harder than it looks," Lila said.

"I'll give you a hand up," Klara offered, reaching for Lila.

"No, thanks. I'm no quitter. I'll keep trying until I learn how to do it. Part of the difficulty is that I'm used to riding a surfboard where both of my feet are free. This snowboard arrangement, with both feet strapped to the board, feels foreign and awkward, and the boots are bulky, too," Lila said, but she stood up on her very next try.

She peered down the slope and looked at Klara with a dubious expression. "It looks like a long way down there."

POP QUIZ

What complaint did Lila have about her boots?

ⓐ They're bulky.
ⓑ They're too tight.

KEY WORDS

- enact
- with ease (= easily)
- success
- give ~ a hand
- quitter

- difficulty
- be used to + *Verb*-ing
  (= be accustomed to + *verb*-ing)
- arrangement
- foreign

- awkward
- bulky
- peer
- dubious
- expression

"Don't worry," Klara said. "We'll start you off with heel sliding first, and get you comfortable with that, and move onto toe sliding. You'll be heading down the slope in no time. First, though, allow me to tell you about falling down, because you will, and you need to do it correctly so you don't hurt yourself." 🌐

"You're teaching me how to wipe out," Lila said, "just like in surfing."

POP QUIZ

Which of the following is similar to wipeout in surfing?

ⓐ falling down
ⓑ standing up

KEY WORDS

- in no time
- correctly
- hurt oneself (hurt-hurt-hurt)
- elbow
- fist
- forearm
- bottom
- immediately

- spread out (spread-spread-spread)
- impact
- obstacle (= obstruction)
- out of the way
- support
- grip
- thigh

"Exactly. If you're falling forward, bring your elbows in close to your body, fist your hands, and fall on your knees and then your forearms.

If you're falling backwards, you'll land on your bottom, but immediately lay back to help spread out the impact. Also, the board can be an obstacle when falling backwards, so lift it up and out of the way with your legs. You may help support the weight by gripping your hands behind your thighs. Any questions?"

"Nope. Let's practice the heel slide. I'm ready to ride!"

"From surfing, you already understand how to shift your body for balance and to direct the board where you want to go. Snowboarding is different, of course, but I believe you'll find some of the mechanics of it to be quite similar." Klara said.

"For heel sliding, face forward so your toes are pointing down the slope and, when the board begins to slide, shift your weight back to your heels to slow yourself down. You see? The more you raise your toes and dig in with your heels, the slower you will go.  As you slide, balance your body over the board with your knees and hips slightly bent, back straight, hands at your sides. Yes!"

Klara cheered when Lila controlled her sliding snowboard as instructed. "To slide back and forth, point your hand in the direction you want to go and shift a bit more weight into that direction. Yes, just like that. You've got it!"

The girls stopped when two snowboarders glided up beside them. It was the same two boys who had stood in line behind them at the chairlift, and Lila wished she could control the blush of her cheeks when the handsome boy with dark hair smiled at her.

"Hello," he said. "My name is Erik, and my friend is Felix."

"Hello," said Felix. He smiled at Klara, who introduced herself and Lila.

POP QUIZ

To practice heel sliding, which direction did Lila face?

ⓐ with her toes pointing down the slope
ⓑ with her toes pointing up the slope

KEY WORDS

- shift
- mechanics
- dig (dig-dug-dug)

- slightly
- control
- instruct

- direction

"We overheard you speaking English and tried to guess where you're from, but it was not easy as you sounded like both American and Australian to us," Erik said.

"Oh, you're right, I'm from America but moved to Australia when I was seven, with my family," Lila answered.

"And this is your first time snowboarding, I'm guessing," Erik said. "I noticed you're learning to heel slide, and that your friend, Klara, is doing a fine job of teaching you. I guess we'll leave you to it. Perhaps we'll see you at the bottom of the slope."

Lila and Klara waved goodbye to Erik and Felix, and the boys sped off down the hill, hot-dogging and obviously showing off for the girls.

"I told you there were cute boys here," Klara said when Erik and Felix disappeared around a curve. "Do you want to practice heel sliding some more, or are you ready to learn to toe slide?"

Lila agreed to the toe sliding lesson, and Klara grinned. "Okay, but first, I want to show you how to roll over. Just do what I do."

POP QuIz

What did the boys do as they sped off down the hill?

ⓐ raced each other to the bottom of the mountain
ⓑ snowboarded fast to show off for the girls

KEY WORDS

- **overhear** (overhear-overheard-overheard)
- **speed off** (speed-speeded/sped-speeded/sped)
- **hot-dog**
- **show off**

- **curve**
- **agree**
- **roll over**

Klara sat down in the snow, facing down the slope. She laid back, and pulled her board over with her as she rolled to her stomach. When she stood up, she was backwards from before, now facing the top of the ski run.

Lila copied Klara, and both of them stood with their backs to the downward slope.

KEY WORDS

▪ downward

▪ distribute

"To toe slide, you'll control your speed by lifting your heels up away from the snow and pushing your toes toward the snow, or let your heels go closer to the snow if you want to go faster. Practice sliding back and forth. Do it the same way you did before, by pointing and distributing a bit of weight into the direction you want to go. Practice until you're comfortable, and when you're ready, we'll ride our boards straight down the hill."

"It seems that the trick to snowboarding is balance."

"Exactly," Klara said, nodding.

Lila practiced the toe slide and learned to turn the board by using both the heel and toe techniques. She experimented with different body movements by shifting her weight. While she practiced, Erik and Felix sped down the hill on their snowboards several more times, and then the boys glided over to the girls again.

"You ready to ride down?" Erik asked, situating his goggles on his forehead and away from his eyes so he could look at Lila directly.

"I think so," Lila said. She looked at Klara and gave her the thumbs-up sign.  "Let's do this!"

▲ "thumb down" and "thumb up"

"All right, then," Klara said. "Start by putting more weight over your lead foot, point your front hand and shoulder downhill, and your back hand and shoulder uphill."

KEY WORDS

- technique
- experiment

- situate
- forehead

- thumbs-up
- uphill (↔ downhill)

"Watch me," said Felix. He demonstrated the instructions
Klara had given to Lila and sped down the slope.

"Since you're riding straight, you can take the pressure off
your heels and toes and let the board slide flat if you want
to. See?" Erik demonstrated as Felix had done and he, too,
sped down the slope, kicking up snow as he went.

"They're showing off again," Klara said, chuckling, and
shook her head.

"Yes, but they're cute." Lila smiled. "And now I must attempt to snowboard down the hill without taking a spectacular tumble and embarrassing myself."

"I think snowboarding is easier than surfing. It's hard to stand up on a surfboard!" Klara said. "When you taught me to surf, it seemed as if all I did was wipe out."

"You learned, though," Lila told her. "And so shall I." 📖 She adjusted her goggles and drew a deep breath. "Here we go!"

POP QUIZ

What word did Lila use to describe Erik and Felix?
ⓐ annoying
ⓑ cute

KEY WORDS

- pressure
- flat
- kick up

- take a tumble
- spectacular
- embarrass

- adjust
- draw a deep breath

Lila directed her snowboard down the slope, and using the techniques as she had been instructed and had practiced, she was able to control her speed, at first being cautious and then picking up speed as her confidence grew.

The wind bit at her face as she snowboarded down the hill, but she felt as if she had learned to fly!

She was quite proud of herself when she glided to the bottom of the downhill run without having fallen even once.

She had traveled rather slowly compared to the others, but she deemed it to be a splendid initial effort and promised herself she'd descend faster on the next run.

Erik and Felix skated over to Lila and Klara with smiles on their faces.

"That was great for your first time downhill," Erik told Lila. "Why don't we all take the lift up together and ride down again?"

Lila glanced at Klara who smiled and nodded. Together, the four of them skated toward the ski lift, and although Lila remained cautious, as she was still a beginner, she knew her confidence and skill would grow.

POP QUIZ

As her confidence grew, Lila picked up _____.

ⓐ snow
ⓑ speed

KEY WORDS

- cautious
- pick up speed
- confidence

- bite (bite-bit-bitten)
- be proud of
- deem

- splendid
- initial
- descend

"I thought snowboarding would be more akin to surfing,"
Lila said after they were seated and the chair began its ascent
up the mountain.

"You can surf?" Erik's dark brows winged upward.

"Yes. I live in Sydney and surf at Manly and Freshwater
beaches all the time but snowboarding is quite different,
while being somewhat similar at the same time." Lila
laughed and shrugged her shoulders. "I know that sounds
like a contradiction, but I'm not sure how else to explain it."

"Surfing is much more difficult," Klara piped in with her opinion. "To begin with, in surfing, there is no chairlift taking you out past the breakers. You must paddle there yourself, which in itself is tiring. And the conditions are constantly changing, unlike snowboarding, where the mountain remains the same, unless weather conditions shift, but then, that doesn't occur without warning. With surfing, you have only a few seconds to perform correctly when the wave comes, but with snowboarding, you can take all day to come down the mountain. Also, when you finally stand up on your surfboard for the first time, you feel as if you're hovering on the edge of a wobbling cliff," Klara said. "I think there is more control with snowboarding."

POP QUIZ

Who was surprised to learn Lila knew how to surf?
ⓐ Felix
ⓑ Erik

KEY WORDS

- be akin to
- wing (= soar, fly)
- upward
- shrug one's shoulders
- contradiction
- pipe in

- to begin with
- in itself
- tiring
- conditions
- constantly
- unlike

- unless
- occur
- warning
- hover

"And there are no sharks swimming on a mountain," Felix joked, and they all laughed.

"There are avalanches, though," Erik said. "A couple of backcountry skiers were injured here at Feldberg a few years ago."

"Here? On this same slope?" Lila asked, alarmed.

KEY WORDS

- avalanche
- backcountry
- be injured
- alarmed

"No." Klara shook her head. "They were off-piste." When Lila's brows drew together in a confused frown, Klara explained, "Backcountry skiers are skiers who ski outside of marked areas, and a piste is a

▲ avalanche

marked ski run. When they were caught in the avalanche, they were off-piste."

"So tell us, Lila, which do you prefer now that you've done both, surfing or snowboarding?" Erik asked as the chairlift delivered them to the top of the run. They stood and skated from the lift.

"It is impossible to say," Lila told him. "I've been surfing since I was seven, and it's in my blood—I can't imagine my life without the ocean and a surfboard." Aha!

POP QUIZ

What is a piste?
ⓐ a ski lift   ⓑ a marked ski run

KEY WORDS

- off-piste
- confused
- frown

- marked
- prefer
- deliver

- impossible (↔ possible)
- in one's blood

She used her heels to stop her forward motion and took a moment to gaze at the breathtaking view from this peak, a panoramic vision of blue skies, white snow, and majestic trees, so different from the vast expanse of ocean she was used to.

"But now that I've learned to snowboard…"

"Yes?" prompted Klara.

"I love this, too." Lila turned to her friend, smiled wide, and shifted her weight.

As the snowboard began to slide downhill and pick up speed, she thought of Emma's words after surfing with Will. It wasn't true only for surfing, she thought, and called out to the treetops, "I'm hooked for life!"

POP QUIZ

What was the last thing that Lila said about snowboarding?

ⓐ "I'm hooked for life!"

ⓑ "Good luck!"

KEY WORDS

- peak
- panoramic
- vision

- majestic
- vast expanse of
- prompt

- treetop

Chapter Two · Comprehension Quiz

 A Mark T for true or F for false.

❶ Klara forgot to teach Lila how to fall down safely. T F

❷ The board can be an obstacle when falling backwards. T F

❸ You use your legs to lift the board up and out of the way. T F

❹ If you land on your bottom, lay back to spread out
the impact. T F

B Choose the best answer to each question.

❶ Why did Lila blush?

a) The dark-haired boy smiled and waved at her.

b) She fell down.

c) The blond boy smiled and waved at her.

d) She tripped getting off the ski lift.

❷ What did Erik and Felix do while Lila practiced toe sliding?

a) watched her practice the whole time

b) waited for her at the bottom of the slope

c) sped down the hill on their snowboards

d) practiced toe sliding with her

C Solve the crossword puzzle.

Across

❸ _____ skiers ski outside of marked areas.

Down

❶ In surfing, there is no _____ taking you out past the breakers.

❷ As the snowboard began to slide _____ and pick up speed, she thought of Emma's words after surfing with Will.

❸ Lila hoped the dark-haired boy couldn't see her _____.

❹ Lila describes Erik and Felix as _____.

Let's Review the Story

Fill in the blanks to review the story.

Title: [_____]

story 1: [_____]

Main characters and their roles: [____] is the surfing student, and [____] is the surfing teacher.

Setting: Freshwater Beach, near Sydney, [____]
Weather: sunny, hot, 23°C

Unexpected event:
Emma was invited to surf [____] with Lila's friend, [____].

story 2: [_____]

Main characters and their roles: [____] is the snowboarding student, and [____] is the snowboarding teacher.

Setting: Feldberg, [____]
Weather: sunny, cold, −4°C

Unexpected event:
Lila and Klara made new friends, E [____] and F [____].

Differences between surfing and snowboarding:

Surfing	Snowboarding
a. You must [____] yourself out past the breakers.	a. A c [____] takes you up the mountain.
b. Weather conditions are constantly [____].	b. Weather conditions remain the [____].
c. You have only a few [____] to perform correctly.	c. You can take [____] [____] to come down the mountain.

Similarities between surfing and snowboarding:
a. Both sports require a b [____].
b. Both sports require a good sense of b [____].
c. Special c [____] are necessary.

Let's Think & Talk

Think about the following questions and answer them freely.

❶ What do surfing and snowboarding have in common? What are the differences? Tell us the similarities and differences between the two sports.

❷ Besides surfing and snowboarding, what other board sports are there? Do some research and tell your friends what you learned.

❸ Surfing and snowboarding are sports that have a lot in common. What other sports have something in common? In addition, explain what it is they have in common.

❹ What is your favorite sport? Explain to your friends why you like the sport, the attractive characteristics of the sport for you, and what precaution you should take when learning the sport.

Let's Review the Story

Title: **Cool Board Sports**

story 1: **Ride the Waves!**

Main characters and their roles:
Emma is the surfing student, and **Lila** is the surfing teacher.

Setting: Freshwater Beach, near Sydney, **Australia**
Weather: sunny, hot, 23°C

Unexpected event:
Emma was invited to surf **tandem** with Lila's friend, **Will**.

story 2: **Fly on the Snow!**

Main characters and their roles:
Lila is the snowboarding student, and **Klara** is the snowboarding teacher.

Setting: Feldberg, **Germany**
Weather: sunny, cold, −4°C

Unexpected event:
Lila and Klara made new friends, **Erik** and **Felix**.

Differences between surfing and snowboarding:

Surfing	Snowboarding
a. You must **paddle** yourself out past the breakers.	a. A **chairlift** takes you up the mountain.
b. Weather conditions are constantly **changing**.	b. Weather conditions remain the **same**.
c. You have only a few **seconds** to perform correctly.	c. You can take **all** **day** to come down the mountain.

Similarities between surfing and snowboarding:
a. Both sports require a **board**.
b. Both sports require a good sense of **balance**.
c. Special **clothes** are necessary.

Smart Readers: **Wise & Wide**

After-reading **Test**

- Cool Board Sports
- Level 6
- 26 Questions

(Vocabulary 5 / Reading Comprehension 16 /

Sentence Structure & Grammar 5)

1. What does "with caution" mean in the following sentence?

   > Klara slid fast on her snowboard, but Lila proceeded <u>with caution</u>.

   ① fearfully   ② momentarily

   ③ carefully   ④ awkwardly

2. What does "bulky" mean in the following sentence?

   > This snowboard arrangement, with both feet strapped to the board, feels foreign and awkward, and the boots are <u>bulky</u>, too.

   ① large and warm
   ② warm and comfortable
   ③ large and clumsy
   ④ heavy and cold

3. What does "competent" mean in the following sentence?

   > Lila said you're a strong and <u>competent</u> swimmer.

   ① skilled   ② unqualified

   ③ vigilant   ④ alarmed

4. What does "deft" mean in the following sentence?

   > In a single <u>deft</u> and graceful motion, Will rose to his feet.

   ① unique and loud
   ② smooth and slow
   ③ skilful and quick
   ④ natural and tough

5. What is the proper word for the blank?

> As her confidence grew, Lila _____ speed.

① picked up   ② turned on

③ pulled up   ④ brought on

6. What did Lila tell Emma and Alec they would walk to see?

① the headland

② the promontory

③ a statue of Sally Fitzgibbons

④ a statue of Duke Kahanamoku

7. Which Australians were surfing before Duke's exhibition?

① Tommy and William Walker

② Doris Stubbins and Mick Fanning

③ William Walker and Isabel Letham

④ Tommy Walker and Isabel Letham

8. How long did Emma practice standing up on her surfboard on the beach?

① until sundown

② until lunchtime

③ until her movements were easy and sure

④ until she didn't make any mistakes

9. What do you use to protect your head when you wipe out?

① a helmet   ② a life jacket

③ a foam board   ④ your arms

10. Why did Will insist Emma wear the life jacket?
    ① to ensure her safety
    ② for buoyancy
    ③ for balance
    ④ so he could help her stand up

11. What did Emma do to help herself balance?
    ① She knelt down.
    ② She spread out her arms.
    ③ She kept her gaze on the beach.
    ④ She wore her rash guard.

12. After her tandem ride, Emma said, "I'm hooked for life!" Who else once said this?
    ① Lila   ② Mick Fanning
    ③ Isabel Letham   ④ Will

13. Compared to surfing, snowboarding requires so much _____.
    ① time   ② effort
    ③ sunscreen   ④ gear

14. What do snowboarding socks, thermal body shirt, and thermal underwear comprise?
    ① the base layer   ② the third layer
    ③ the second layer   ④ the thermal layer

15. Which foot gets strapped into the front binding before skating?
    ① the free foot
    ② the lead foot
    ③ neither foot is strapped in
    ④ either foot can go in front

16. Why did Lila compare Felix and Erik to salt and pepper?
    ① They were always together.
    ② One was blond and the other dark-haired.
    ③ They had opposite personalities.
    ④ One wore light-colored clothing and the other wore dark clothing.

17. To what did Lila compare the sparkling snow?
    ① crystals   ② silver
    ③ diamonds   ④ glitter

18. What did the girls do to ensure their snowboards didn't slide away?
    ① They sat on top of the snowboards.
    ② They put the snowboards on their laps.
    ③ They attached the leashes on the snowboards to their ankles.
    ④ They turned the boards upside down with the bindings in the snow.

19. Where were Lila's toes pointing when she practiced heel sliding?
    ① up the slope   ② down the slope
    ③ inward   ④ outward

20. What was the first thing Klara did when teaching Lila to roll over with the snowboard?
    ① She sat down in the snow facing down the slope.
    ② She knelt in the snow facing down the slope.
    ③ She sat down in the snow facing up the slope.
    ④ She knelt in the snow facing up the slope.

21. Lila said she must attempt to snowboard down the hill without taking a "spectacular tumble." What did she mean by this?
    ① losing her snowboard
    ② falling down and looking foolish
    ③ bumping into other snowboarders
    ④ falling from the ski lift

※ Choose the wrong part of each sentence. (22~23)

22.
There was <u>no</u> <u>deny</u> she'd <u>rather</u> be <u>at</u> the beach.
          ①   ②   ③   ④

23.
Will is <u>one</u> of my surfing <u>instructor</u>, and he <u>does</u> <u>competitive</u> surfing.
      ①   ②   ③   ④

※ Choose the correct word for each blank. (24~25)

24.
Those will be the easiest _____ you to ride.

    ① to   ② for
    ③ with   ④ on

25.

> As _____ as you're brave on the ski slopes, that's all that matters.

① many   ② much
③ long   ④ big

26. What is the correct sentence?
     ① It was long before Herr Reinhart, Klara's father, had parked the SUV.
     ② It wasn't long before Herr Reinhart, Klara's father, had parked the SUV.
     ③ It was long after Herr Reinhart, Klara's father, had parked the SUV.
     ④ It wasn't long after Herr Reinhart, Klara's father, had parked the SUV.

Lisa Ricard Claro
Lisa Ricard Claro is an award-winning short story author with published articles and stories spanning multiple media, including two adult fiction novels and a third scheduled for publication. She resides in Atlanta, Georgia with her husband, two dogs and two cats, and dreams of one day living at the beach. Writing is Lisa's passion, and she loves creating fiction and nonfiction stories for both adults and children.

 Smart Readers
Wise & Wide 6-5

Cool Board Sports

Written by Lisa Ricard Claro
Illustrated by Hyeyeong Kim

First Published in August 2016

Editorial Manager: Juyon Choi
Editors: Juyon Choi, Hyunjeong Kim, Kyunghee Jang, Jiyeong Park
Designers: Eunhee Lee, Elim
Cover Designer: Eunhee Lee

Published and distributed by

 Happy House

Darakwon Bldg., 64-1 Jandari-ro, Mapo-gu, Seoul, Korea 04031
Tel: 82-2-736-2031(ext. 250)   Fax: 82-2-732-2037
Homepage: www.ihappyhouse.co.kr
Publisher: Kyudo Chung

Copyright © Darakwon Publishing Company 2016
English Edition published 2016, by arrangement with Darakwon, by Happy House
English Edition Copyright © 2016, Happy House

ISBN: 978-89-6653-412-8 18740 / 978-89-6653-156-1 18740(set)

[Components]
• 1 Audio CD (Recording Studio: Aram)
• Answer Keys & Korean Translation: Free download at www.ihappyhouse.co.kr